Time Pieces for Cello

VOLUME 3

Arranged by Catherine Black & Paul Harris

ABRSM

Printed on materials from sustainable sources

CONTENTS

Time Pieces for Cello

Volume 3

For Christopher Bunting

1567 Melody in the Third Mode

Thomas Tallis
(*c.*1505–1585)

Published by ABRSM (Publishing) Ltd, a wholly owned subsidiary of ABRSM
© 1997 by The Associated Board of the Royal Schools of Music

AB 2579

<u>1691</u> Fairest Isle

from *King Arthur*

Henry Purcell
(1659–1695)

4

1724 Adoring I suffer

from *Julius Caesar in Egypt*

George Frideric Handel
(1685–1759)

AB 2579

1725 Bist du bei mir

Gottfried Heinrich Stölzel
(1690–1749)

AB 2579

1740 Blow, blow thou Winter wind

Thomas Arne
(1710–1778)

1755 Minuet
from Concerto Grosso in B minor

William Boyce
(1711–1779)

AB 2579

1762 Dance of the Blessed Spirits

from *Orfeo*

Christoph von Gluck
(1714–1787)

1795 Andante

from Sonata in G, Op. 12

Carl Sigmund Schönebeck
(1758–c.1800)

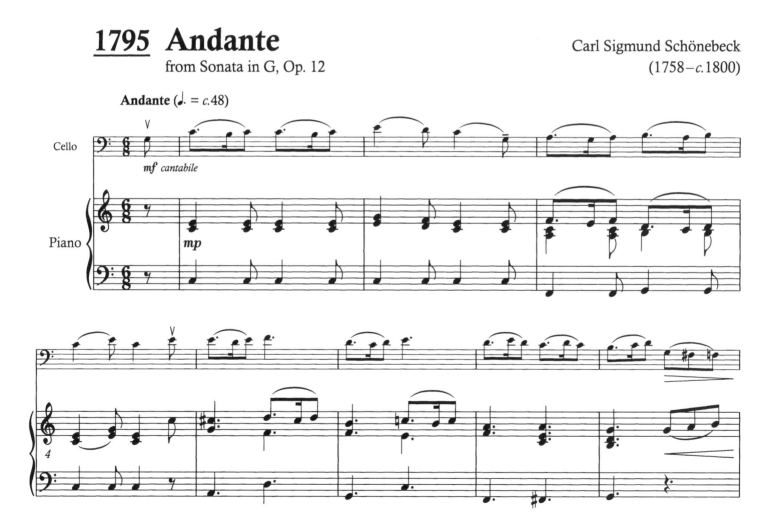

Fine

AB 2579

1848 Humming Song

from *Album for the Young*

Robert Schumann
(1810–1856)

AB 2579

Time Pieces for Cello

Volume 3

For Christopher Bunting

1567 Melody in the Third Mode

Thomas Tallis
(*c.*1505–1585)

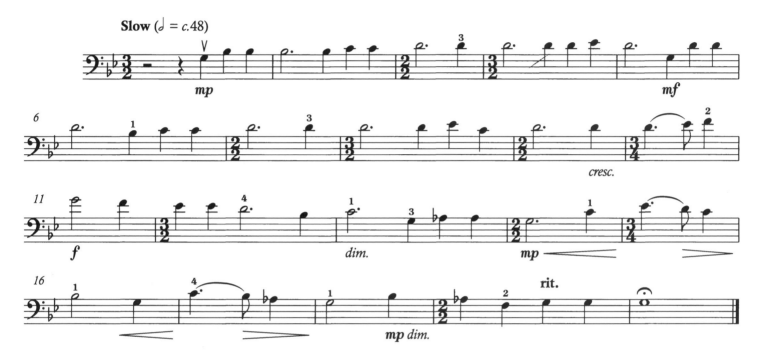

1691 Fairest Isle

from *King Arthur*

Henry Purcell
(1659–1695)

AB 2579

1724 Adoring I suffer

from *Julius Caesar in Egypt*

George Frideric Handel
(1685–1759)

1725 Bist du bei mir

Gottfried Heinrich Stölzel
(1690–1749)

Andante (♩ = c.72)

1740 Blow, blow thou Winter wind

Thomas Arne
(1710–1778)

Andante con moto (♩ = c.120)

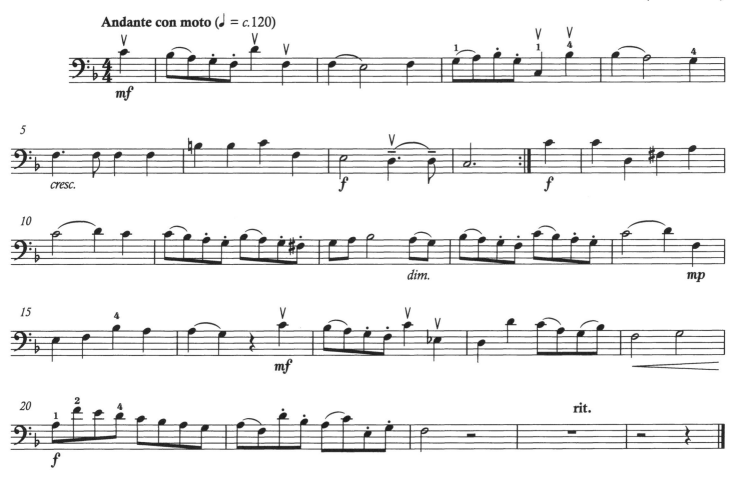

1755 Minuet

from Concerto Grosso in B minor

William Boyce
(1711–1779)

AB 2579

1762 Dance of the Blessed Spirits

from *Orfeo*

Christoph von Gluck
(1714–1787)

1795 Andante

from Sonata in G, Op. 12

Carl Sigmund Schönebeck
(1758–*c.*1800)

D.C. al Fine

1848 Humming Song

from *Album for the Young*

Robert Schumann
(1810–1856)

1867 Softly awakes my heart

from *Samson et Dalila*

Camille Saint-Saëns
(1835–1921)

1871 Humoreske

Pyotr Ilyich Tchaikovsky
(1840–1893)

AB 2579

1885 On a tree by a river

from *The Mikado*

Arthur Sullivan
(1842–1900)

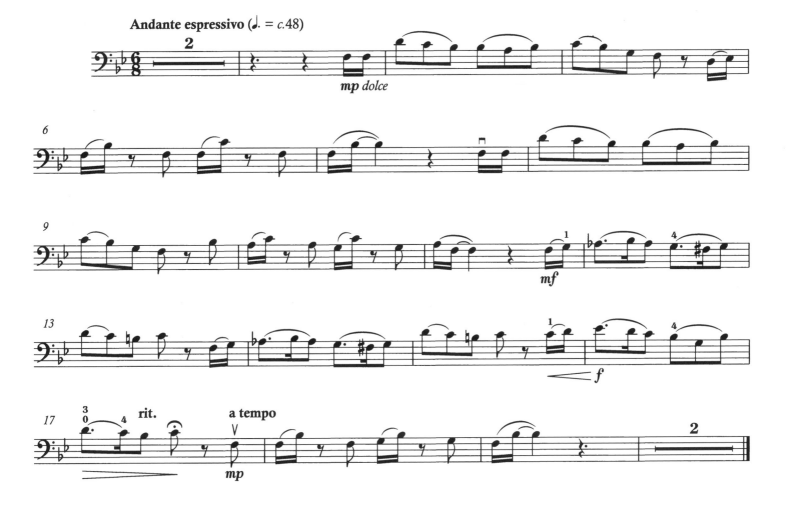

*c.*1896 Dedication

Enrique Granados
(1867–1918)

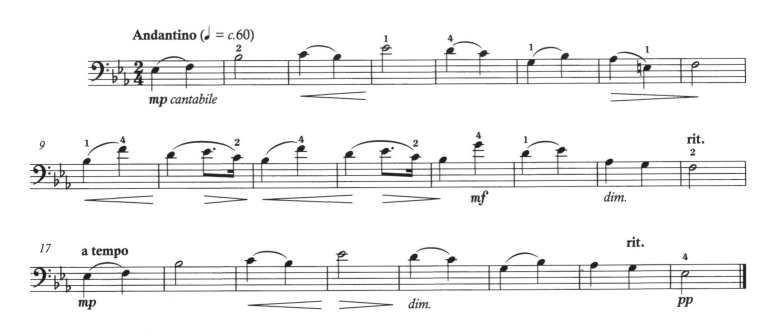

1902 Je te veux

Erik Satie
(1866–1925)

AB 2579

1943 For the flowers are great blessings

from *Rejoice in the Lamb*

Benjamin Britten
(1913–1976)

AB 2579

1996 Black and White Blues

Paul Harris

Music origination by
Barnes Music Engraving Ltd, East Sussex
Printed by Caligraving Limited Thetford Norfolk England

AB 2579

12:16

LEFT HAND ON "C" STRING

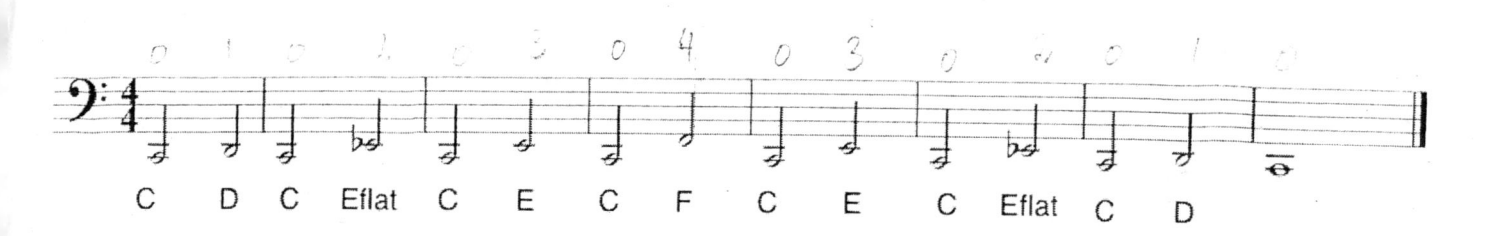

C D C Eflat C E C F C E C Eflat C D

Frère Jacques

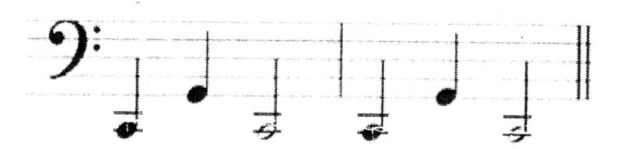

1867 Softly awakes my heart

from *Samson et Dalila*

Camille Saint-Saëns
(1835–1921)

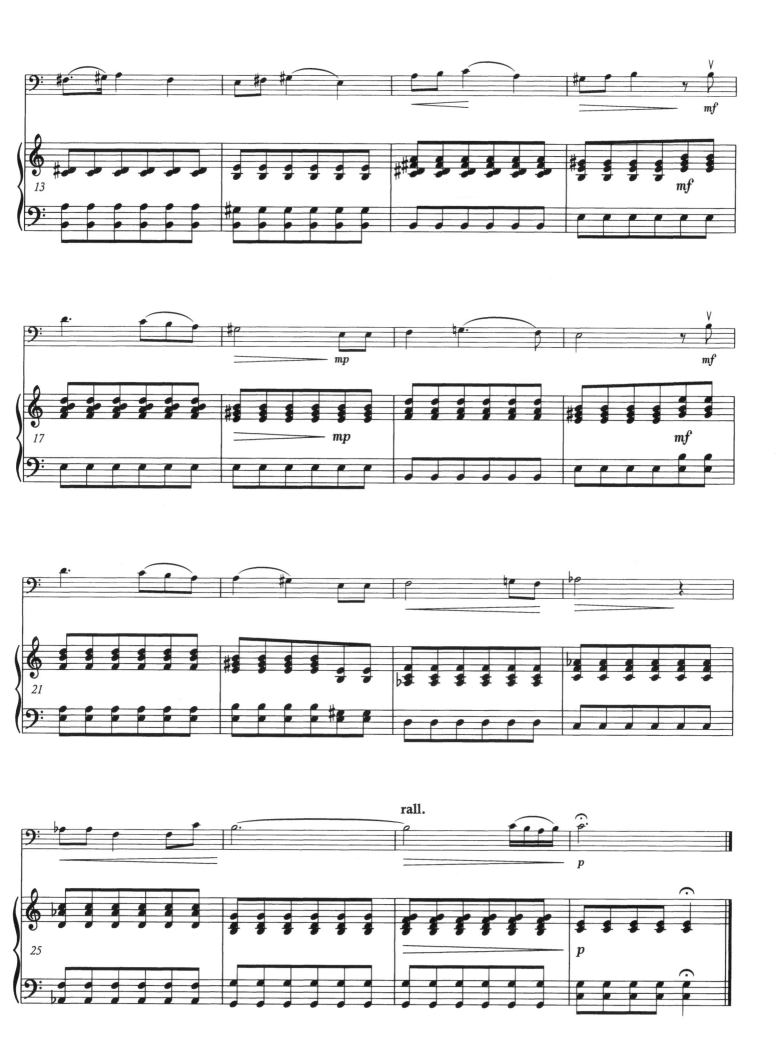

1871 Humoreske

Pyotr Ilyich Tchaikovsky
(1840–1893)

poco meno mosso

semplice, ma espressivo

D.C. al Fine

1885 On a tree by a river

Arthur Sullivan
(1842–1900)

from *The Mikado*

*c.*1896 **Dedication**

Enrique Granados
(1867–1918)

AB 2579

1902 Je te veux

Erik Satie
(1866–1925)

1943 For the flowers are great blessings

from *Rejoice in the Lamb*

Benjamin Britten
(1913–1976)

1996 Black and White Blues

Paul Harris

Music origination by
Barnes Music Engraving Ltd, East Sussex
Printed by Caligraving Limited Thetford Norfolk England